CONTROLLING ANXIETY AND PANIC ATTACKS

Immediate help with heart palpitations, anxiety, panic and more. How to improve your quality of life. Help yourself and your family members, who suffer from these orders. Accept, reprogram mind and gain calm and control in times of stress.

Tips and therapies. Also, Alternatives to pharmacology.

HENRY BISHOP

Copyright © 2020

DISCLAIMER 5

INTRODUCTION 6

CHAPTER ONE... 11

SELF-EVALUATION 11

CHAPTER TWO...16

PRIORITIZE YOUR LIST 16

CHAPTER THREE 20

PLACING YOUR CHALLENGES INTO CATEGORY 20

CHAPTER FOUR...30

CHANGE BEGINS WITH ME 30

CHAPTER FIVE..41

NEVER ALLOW YOUR PAST AFFECT YOUR PRESENT 41

CHAPTER SIX 50

IDENTIFY YOUR EXCESSIVE MEMORY 50

CHAPTER 7 58

MINDFULNESS 58

CHAPTER 8 66

PRACTICING INTO PERFECTION 66

CONCLUSION 72

Disclaimer

All knowledge contained in this book is given for informational and educational purposes only. The author is not in any way accountable for any results or outcomes that emanate from using this material. Constructive attempts have been made to provide information that is both accurate and effective, but the author is not bound for the accuracy or use/misuse of this information.

Introduction

In the United States, anxiety and antidepressants will always be on the list in the last few decades if you have to look at the ten most prescribed drugs in the country. This is not an accident, nor is it madness.

We live in a very stressful world. In fact, many Americans struggle with anxiety disorders at one level or another. There may be different manifestations, but don't be fooled that this inevitably affects a more efficient life.

Do you want to be more successful in your relationship or just want to be a happier person or you want to be more effective in your career? It is of importance that you consider facing your fears head on. Unfortunately, this is easier said than done because most people deal with fear the wrong way. This eventually leads to regrettable and unforgettable consequences.

If you read through this book, you might face fear at one level or another, or you have a loved one, please understand that this book teaches you alternatives that will help you overcome your fears. However, fear is a combination of your environment, your genetic predisposition, and the coping mechanism you choose to live with.

Never underestimate the control you have over the situations you find yourself. Many people feel that if they have a genetic predisposition to all types of diseases, they generally do not have an opinion about what is bothering them.

In other words, they really have no choice in their situation. That's a shame because the billion-dollar pharmaceutical industry will benefit tremendously if people continue to believe they have no choice or alternatives. Because if there is no individual control over fear and this is only a definite conclusion and you can only provide counseling regarding psychopharmaceutical interventions, there really isn't much you can do. You really don't have much choice.

Please understand that you have more control and say more than you think you can. Please understand that I am not saying that you should not accept professional help with psychiatric or psychological counseling. I'm not saying that at all.

I suggest you work with a professional, but please understand that you can add to what he gives you or prescribe things that you can do yourself. This is a strategy for rearranging your mindset that allows you to stay in control of your life.

The reason you struggle with fear is because you feel like things are out of control, beyond the reach. You feel like you're living in a world that you haven't created, and for various reasons something is wrong, or you are struggling with guilt, regret, doubt, and other negative emotions about the past.

Please understand that the past has passed. These facts have already happened. It's not like jumping into a time machine and turning things around.

Here are the facts. It has happened, there really isn't much you can do. This milk is spilled. If you are worried about the future, there really isn't anything to worry about because things haven't happened. You are then afforded the opportunity to make things happen. The thing that you fear will be revealed and long forgotten.

The only choice you truly have is to grapple with your thoughts here and now. The more you control your current thinking, the better your relationship with your past, and the better you can face the future in this case.

In this book, you will learn how to deal with anxiety and fear without drugs, without professional and expensive psychiatric counseling. I will provide you with how you can easily rearrange your "mental and emotional furniture", hereby controlling your physical disposition.

Chapter One

Self-Evaluation

Name all the things that make you afraid.

You really can't say what it is exactly, but whatever it is, it bothers you. You might not want to define it as fear, but it leaves you emotionally down. As long as you can pinpoint them, write down everything that you are aware of that makes you afraid, you are good to go.

Write down everything you can possibly think of that you fear. It is only once it's written down that we can easily identify what frightens us and what could possibly trigger those feelings of fear. We will only go through a self-examination mode that uses strong emotions or strong feelings as a guide.

In this case, list all the things that you fear.

List everything that bothers you.

There are no wrong or right answers about what bothers you here. If you find what bothers or frightens you irrational or unrealistic, just keep it on the list. It's not like anyone will read through your answers though.

The key here is to help you get a complete picture of the things that could weigh and hold you down emotionally. Mention the things that you always blame or use as excuses. These are the things that you are worried about. It could be those things that you have done or said in the past that still scares the hell out of you. Write everything down in one piece. As long as you can remember it now, it's good enough to put it on the list.

Write down things that you doubt.

Do you have a relationship that you doubt? Do you feel you don't love your parents? Do you feel your parents don't love you? Do you feel that you really don't believe in your parents' religion or the religion you choose, or do you have little faith in your partner?

Whatever it is, write down those things that you doubt. Put down into writing as many of the things you doubt as you can get yourself to remember. There are no right or wrong answers like I said earlier on. So write it all down without leaving anything out. Remember no one will review your answers. It is important that you get everything you can think of down, as long as it crossed your mind.

Don't edit what you have written. Think clearly about what happened. As long as it comes to your mind and you can clearly describe it, write it down as it is. Don't edit it. Don't tone it down and don't add to it what you don't doubt.

Take your time to write a complete list

If you need a few days or even a week or two to write all that gives you emotional hiccups, that's fine. Take your time to write them out. Give yourself time to write a complete list of all the things that you are worried about. It is important to note that you don't need to force yourself to write, instead allow it to come to you easily. Don't think this should be a deliberate, pre-planned, compulsory and very calculated exercise. This defeats the purpose.

The point here is to make a complete list of your fears, anxiety and in fact your emotional problems without stress. To do this, you must be completely free and flexible within yourself as much as possible. Unfortunately, if you overwork yourself you are less likely to make changes.

A better approach is to write all these things up as if you were taking a bath. Do you remember the last time you showered and got this idea? Yeah, people do it all the time. When they take a shower, they don't try to think in one particular way or direction. They allow the train of their thoughts to just flow without cease. They are more susceptible to true insights and flashes of intuition. Take a cue from this and allow yourself to freely remember the needed information.

Chapter TWO

Prioritize your List

Sort your list by intensity. Read through your list and arrange details by how emotionally intense they are. When you think of a father you never knew because he left you when you were still in the womb or when you were still a child, how do you feel about that? How strong are your emotions? What feelings do you have?

Do this for everything that you have registered. This will take time. It's easy to see what you write at face value. It's tempting to think that it is when you remember certain memories as emotionally intense, you might want to do things differently.

Pamper yourself with emotional thoughts and feelings. How intense was that? Is it consistently high? Are you sure it's not just a one-time problem? Are you sure you don't remember the memory? They can be very difficult.

When you think about these memories, emotions must surely come to mind. You cannot imagine being angry with this memory in the past. That should not be the case. It must be an emotionally direct experience.

Take time to measure the intensity precisely. Take time to examine each item as each has its own emotional impact on you. After taking the time to adequately assess or evaluate the emotional intensity of your memory, you need to take extra steps. This are very important step.

Avoid the tendency to read the intensity of your emotions. In simple language, this means that emotions in themselves must be strong. When you think of something, strong emotions must appear in your head.

Avoid thinking about situations where when you think about something, then the fact that you think about it and feel bad in your memory makes you feel intense emotions. The intense emotions that you experience are actually not about memories themselves, but about actions turning into memories.

Do you see the difference? One of these situations is related to the actual fact of memory. The other is just your interpretation of these facts. There is a big difference between the two.

Be honest

Please understand that you are not out to impress anyone here. Try as much as possible not to prove anything to anyone. You are not trying to be a role model to anyone, it's just yourself alone.

Since nobody will see your list, it's important for you to be honest with yourself. Because if you are not honest or restrained, you are the only person who will eventually suffer the consequence. So be honest in terms of prioritizing and assessing this problem.

Chapter Three

Placing your challenges into Category

Begin to categorize your fears, with the strongest fears falling into same category. Can you come up with a broad topic that unites them? Have these things happened in the past? Do you regret these things? Do these things involve people who make you responsible for many things that are wrong in your life? Are these things that you consider part of your personal weaknesses things that make you vulnerable? Think about it.

The key here is to make a clear picture or box for each list you have. And the more you browse through your list, the more this model will appear to fall in place.

Categorize all your Anxiety

This will take time, but you must group all the problems that you have listed based on the problems that you have identified.

I must admit that creating categories for the memories and emotions you have can be very confusing. Therefore, it is a good idea to combine various problems identified into the categories. Please understand that there is no perfect category that fits most of your emotional experiences.

Just don't hesitate and be random to find new categories that are more meaningful. Feel free to create new categories. Don't automatically assume that this is the only way, because many people believe that certain memories must be categorized in certain ways.

If you make it task free, certain pairs can be displayed. You might be able to identify new categories that you have never thought of before.

You don't need to feel pressurized if you just keep all of your memories or all of your gathered

 data in one box. That is the key. Don't feel pressured. It will also be very helpful if you classify your emotional memories as "right" or "wrong". Remember they are yours. You have the right worldwide to classify it because it makes sense to you. That is the key. This is so because you do that to help yourself. Don't do this to impress others. Don't do this because this is homework being evaluated. It must make sense that you can help yourself with your fear and anxiety problem.

Feel free to write down the same fears among various fields. It can be something that has happened in the past that you cannot forget. This is also a cause of regret and also experience of violence.

In this case, place this experience in three areas. Write down and classify the intensity of fear that you have divided into several topics. Manage your concern for the best of everyone's abilities.

That will not be easy because when we think of traumatic incidents, we are often hit by tsunamis. Our emotions get better and it looks very strong when compared to other fears we have and when we have them.

From the perspective of the big picture, it turns out that the fear that appears so strong and extraordinary is actually quite calm. So you must have a good picture perspective if you classify all of these problems on each topic.

If you believe you will achieve it

Please understand that faith is the foundation of your life. If you believe a thing, you will achieve it, and if you don't believe this will be a much more difficult path for you. This does not exactly mean that you will fail, but it will be more difficult for you to get what you want without believing.

You must have your mindset in the right place before starting this journey to overcome your fears. If not put in the right place, your thoughts will sabotage, undermine, and constantly hinder you. Before you realize it, you only lose your enthusiasm because of your negative thoughts.

How does thinking affect your reality? Believe it or not, your thoughts help you work on reality. When your thoughts are well placed, they help you grasp hold of reality.

We are all editors of our personal reality. Just because most of us don't take full responsibility for it doesn't negate this fact. We all have this ability to edit relevant parts of reality away. This is how it works in reality. Believe it or not, you choose it at some point. It might not look like that, but rightly so it was chosen all the same by you. You will not hold on to your opinion unless you have chosen it. This mindset is not neutral. When you take all these objective stimuli from around the world, you process them through your mind and give them meaning. This is called analysis.

This might look natural, this might be an objective reality, but don't be too confident. This is subjective because two people with two different attitudes see the exact same facts and can go far with two very different conclusions. That is the power of the human mind.

Your childhood, the way you were raised, how people treated you, what violence you suffered, what beliefs you had - all of this influenced your thinking. And that is yours, it is quite different from that of others.

Do you process reality through the lens of your mind and know what is happening? It is true. Your emotional state is affected. This makes you react in a certain way to what happens.

How can it be? If you take action, there are consequences. There is always an end result for every action. The reality of things works like this. So, if you adopt a certain mindset, regardless of whether you realize it or not, you will get a certain reality. And all that is a choice.

As long as you don't take full ownership of your life you will continue to be the person who keeps asking, "What happened?" instead of those who make things happen. Your life is a product of your thinking and so you must think about being responsible for your life. The fact that you are very concerned and feel guilty about certain things or ashamed of certain things is ultimately your choice.

Please understand that I do not blame the victims of violent or negative situations here. Maybe someone sexually harasses you, maybe you become a victim of some crime, maybe someone else has it for you and hurts you, that's not the point. How you react to these events is your responsibility because the same traumatic event can occur to two completely different persons and they can have two completely different reactions.

I know it's a simplification, but that's the truth. Your mindset plays a big role in the perception of global stimuli. Your mindset plays a role in how you understand and accept reality. You have to take it. You must be brave, honest and sincere as you accept what has chosen to happen in your life. Stop blaming others and face the reality.

When you blame others for something wrong in your life, or worse, your personal mistakes, you are basically giving them control of your life. Think of it this way: if your father abandoned you as a child or your mother abused you as a child and caused all your problems, who could finally fix it? This does not take rocket science to fathom. It should be clear enough that only you can fix it.

Let's put it this way: if you go to the store and break something, who should fix it, you or the shopkeeper. Here's a hint: this is not a shopkeeper. Do you see how it works? Because others who you accuse to this day have "ruined your life", then logically they are the only ones who can improve your life? First they break you down, establishing problems to be fixed. This is the problem. These people have lived their lives or are already dead. You are left alone.

They have moved on. If you continue to wait for them to come into your life to bring everything together, all you have to do is prepare for failure. This is what happens when you blame others.

You keep saying: "I am not responsible because that person did it at the time" or "This situation happened to me." Now, this is the most helpless thing you can do for yourself because you put solutions for everything that is wrong with your life in the hands of people or situations that you cannot control.

It's hard enough to change yourself. Can you imagine changing other people? Can you imagine getting them back to your life to change your life?

Big opportunities. They forged ahead. You have changed. You must take responsibility. You must take ownership. You must take the initiative.

I know it hurts because it is so unfair. But do you know what? Life is not fair. You must take this step. You must take responsibility for your life by saying, "It might not be my fault that this happened, but I accept it as my responsibility for myself how I process this information."

In other words, you stop blaming others and take full responsibility for what happens in your life.

CHAPTER FOUR

CHANGE BEGINS WITH ME

You must be committed to changing your mindset. If you change your mindset, everything I will discuss, including overcoming fear, is possible and very possible. You must be ready to make the emotional and psychological improvements needed to fundamentally change the way you see reality, how you carry yourself, and how you treat others.

In other words, you are trying to live a new life that is more successful. But it all starts with your decision to change your mindset.

How important is the decision?

You must understand that there are big differences in how you make real decisions and how to make choices.

Too many people confuse the two. They think that if they really make a decision, they made a choice. You are not there yet. Many other things are still to be considered here. They still consider various factors, but they have already made a decision in their heads.

That is why many people who think they have a solution fail because they never made a decision. When you choose, your mind is bound to certain results. Choices also set your emotional state for certain problems with your decision about the problem. In this mental state, nothing is desired. You are locked and your motivation is activated. You are pumped for that decision.

Now you might think that after this decision point, all magical things will happen if you assume that you have reached the real decision point. I hope it's that easy. Decisions are only the first step. If you really make a decision, that means you are still committed.

How important is that? You know that if you continue to invest time and work, you will get engaged even if you don't like it. You know you are involved when you face one difficulty after another and all kinds of unexpected events happen, and you still do it anyway. This is the power of bonding. No matter how big, this can only be triggered after you make a decision. Both go hand in hand.

Changing your mindset is not easy. We all have our respective habits. Even if we commit to change, our old habits and patterns sometimes begin to show up. But you must stay focused and use your determination to overcome your habits.

Concentrate on what you can get out from your situation. Concentrate on your relief that you can turn away from things that now make you frustrated, sad, mad, and angry. If you focus on what you want to win, it might too difficult, too far, and unachievable. Do the exact opposite, focus on the pain of staying where you are and not changing. You will be left with no choice but to move forward.

You know, there are basically two types of people in this world. On the one hand, there are people who are interested in achievements and the best things in life. In other words, they use their desires to motivate themselves. On the other hand, there are people who lift their fingers to change things when they feel they have lost everything. In other words, they are motivated by fear.

Here's the good news: there are no right or wrong answers. It doesn't matter if you are motivated by your hopes, dreams and highest values or driven by your fears and uncertainties. The most important thing is to put your feet directly in front and continue towards your goal.

So focus on what motivates you and make those changes. Dedicate yourself to thinking and changing your mind and outlook. Make a series of confirmations. This can be in form of short statements

 that you say to yourself non-verbally, but as clearly as possible per day. It might seem silly, but confirmation works.

Why?

They function as a conscious reprogramming of your personal history. If you have problems in any area of your life, it's because you have a personal story that makes this struggle possible.

For example, if you struggle to fulfill your commitments, you might be working on a personal story that tells you that you are not a very trustworthy person or that you are too busy to commit. You really can't keep your word because you have so many other things. You too are a victim deep down.

Affirmations work because it allows you to deliberately think of new programs or descriptions. The more often you repeat it, the more likely it is to sink and become part of your conscious thinking. This doesn't work overnight, but through targeted and committed repetition you get to your choice destination.

Starting a personal change log seems to be an easy ministerial task. After all, just record your personal journey to transformative change. At a certain level, it seems like not much happens. It even seems like you are just going through the motions, or worse, just wasting your time. You need to get this negative thoughts out of your head because starting and keeping a personal change diary can really change you as you try to direct your train of thoughts so you don't worry every day.

When you see how you started and how you think, as well as your description of your personal world and compare it to what you have become, you cannot help but feel motivated. Imagine when you started this process, you might think that your worries and fears are basically you, you feel trapped. You feel like you can't get out of this situation because you just survived. That is you, it is rooted in you as a person deep down. However, if you look at the next entry and find that your thinking has changed, it gives you hope.

Everything might not yet be as desirable as you hope it would be, but it turns out that everything is not as bad as you imagine. This gives you a good reason to move forward. Of course, the change isn't that dramatic, but you don't have to be a hero. The fact that you have changed one bit is good enough to give you hope. This allows you to recover.

Please remember that the key is to change your thinking so that you are less anxious and less frightened and more effective than being merely involved.

The good news is that it doesn't take much to encourage your involvement. All it takes is a simple change. Look for this change. Identify and track these changes by launching and managing a personal change log. Recommend this project to change your mindset every day. Celebrate the power of daily involvement.

The problem with many people who are committed to certain changes in their lives is that they already feel committed. Finally, they think in their minds: "Yes, I do the same thing every day, right? Isn't that an obligation?

To some extent, they are absolutely right. But to begin this process and unleash the power of this daily decision to take a number of actions, regardless of our feelings and what is happening around us, a little awareness is needed. By simply saying "I am committed today" to yourself and then saying the same thing the next day along with its meaning, you align your conscious skills with the side you normally do.

This gives you more power. It also wakes you up or reminds you of your purpose.

Remember that you are trying to change your mindset. You are trying to do something that is very difficult to do. Usually it takes a big disaster for people to change their mindset on something very good. Beyond this relatively rare situation, people stick to their thinking. If you are working on something great it is important you must know this process as well as possible to be able to attack with full force. Challenge your thoughts every day and make a difference.

Communication with difficult people is frustrating and can be like a waste of time. But this can also be a good opportunity to test whether you are making progress in changing your mindset. Remember that you do not change these people. That is not the point. The point is whether the people who threw you or upset you no longer do it because that is the only way to find out if you really changed something about yourself.

You can give yourself all kinds of confirmations and think of warm, blurry images about the change you want to make. Until you actually drag it into a situation that usually challenges you emotionally, you won't make real progress. So find this challenge.

I know that most people will find this situation very difficult, but that is why you have to look for challenges because they really push you to the limit of your ability. You will not grow without experiencing some level of pain. You will not grow without challenges. It will be very difficult for you to change if you are not in a situation where you feel uncomfortable.

Make a list of changes in your thinking

Do you automatically stop blaming others? Have you stopped blaming yourself and feeling guilty automatically? Are you more proactive? Are you more willing to assert yourself? Are you more likely to speak your mind? What changes did you see?

If you don't see enough change, challenge yourself more. Put yourself in situations that normally bother you, hurt you emotionally, and see if you can survive and overcome them. Remember, this is a trial with fire, because baby steps don't work for most people. They hold back and stop growing.

You must commit to this. Victory is about consistency and It. It doesn't matter how many times you think you have failed. What's important is that you jump back when you figuratively collapsed. Of course, it hurts the first time and you might want to stay on the ground, but get stand up back and get used to it. Fasten your belts and before you realize it, you reach the point where you strike and look back. This is called emotional item. This means that you stay on your path no matter what. And this is a sign of maturity and progress.

Chapter Five

Never allow your past affect your present

Too many people are determined by their past. They are very bad and believe that their only value for humanity is that they mess it up. They think that's what makes them special. They think that they really can't overcome this.

Maybe you went to jail. Maybe you are accused of doing something wrong. Maybe you did something for someone else that you already regret. You may have been abused and feel small, helpless, and weak. Whatever happens to you, please understand that this is the past.

Past is past

The past is past and long gone. You don't have a time machine to jump in and change the facts. These facts have happened. Your job now is to live your life so that you are happy, balanced, efficient, loving and friendly. In other words, you are to live for today. Unfortunately, you don't do this if you worry about the past and burn a lot of emotional energy and think about what could happen, what should happen or what will happen.

The more you think about the people you hurt, the worse they are, the stronger the pain, and that poisons your relationships and thoughts today. You are not responsible for doing it. You don't control when you do this.

You must decide to deal with the past. Every few days, you must open a diary for the previous event and then go through the following process. You owe it to yourself. You must be consistent to get out of the burden of the past.

Ask yourself if the past trauma that you remember actually happened. There is something like fake memory. In fact, false memories are constantly implanted. If you don't believe that false memory is possible, think of the 90s. In the 1990s, there were all kinds of scandals in the United States where therapists brought false memories to their patients or clients. This is due to the fact that the people are very impressive.

If you find someone you trust mainly because of the position or authority they have, you are in a very vulnerable position. They are in a position where they can easily influence you.

Many free counseling and psychiatric sessions existed in the 1990s, but there was no clear protocol about suggestibility. Not surprisingly, there are all kinds of wrong memories in this climate because therapists who emphasize or suggest certain associations have created suggestive and false associations in the minds of patients.

Imagine growing up in a family that everyone loves themselves and the understanding is great. You really respect your father and mother, but later on, if you experience alcohol addiction or have problems in your marriage, you will then go to see a therapist. The therapist then guides you through a reckless and unstructured process where you have wrong memories about violence against your parents or partner. How can you regain connection with your parents and partner when you have this false memory that he raped you as a child?

Do you see how this was a problem in the 1990s and it still is a problem today? False memories are more common than we think. Be careful of them.

Question all your memories.

Human memory can actually be very wrong. We often remember things through relationships. When we find someone or an event that is somehow related to the things we remember in the past, our memories grow and we create an entirely new story. It turns out that what we thought was far from it.

So you wonder if it really happened when you saw all the past traumatic events that you prioritized in your diary? Ask yourself as best as you can according to your knowledge and beliefs, is it really happening? That means you are there. You hear something, you smell something, you see something, you touch something, or you feel something.

In other words, with your five senses, you can see that this is a reality. If not, can someone else confirm that this has happened to you? Do you know someone near you who can tell you, "Yes, that happened?

I see it with my own eyes "or" I was there, I watched it all "or" I heard him say that "or" I heard Mother tell you about it "and so on and so forth.

Eliminate the wrong experience

If you cannot find documentary evidence or do not have personal memories of an event and cannot find confirmation from others, decide once and for all that these events did not occur. The next time you remember, say it boldly, slowly, silently: "This is wrong." "That is wrong." "This is not a real memory.

I do not want anything to do with it."

By doing this, you do not belong to the normal wave or chain reaction of negative emotions you feel.

Why waste a lot of emotional and psychological resources on things that haven't happened yet? It might look artificial, it might even look like you just split into the ocean, and it's really useless and meaningless, but you need to repeat the pattern above until it makes sense.

This is an important part of fully retrieving your false memories. If you are not enthusiastic yet, just think of the misery you experience while maintaining false memories. They make you feel small, you lose trust in others, and you feel weak. It's not a good place to be.

Tie this negative emotional state together with the alternative to not repeating the memory ownership statement. Of course, it might seem boring, useless and ineffective to keep repeating this statement, but what else do you have? You really can't say that what you have now will be much better.

The reason why you are reading this book is because you want to get out of all the fears, anxieties, and negative emotions created by false memories. Bad memories are unfortunate, so focus on them.

Tell yourself, "Well, that might repeat itself, it might look mechanical, deep down I feel like I'm just wasting my time, but what do I really have as an alternative? Do I really want to go back to the misery that brought me the wrong memories? "When you paint everything so well, this contrast emphasizes the value of your work.

I know that you may have a million or more other things that you want to follow. We are all busy.

But believe me, if you remember your wrong memories and repeat this claim, you will begin to get your life back. This action is an investment in a better life.

That is not Denial

Please understand that you don't practice rejection. Instead, you only make sense of your situation. If you haven't seen it and no one else has seen it, that practically never happened.

Why do you have to keep fighting for something that didn't happen? That is a discovery. And for some reason you have been stuck in this fiction for years.

Maybe I helped you explain your situation, maybe you gave many reasons, maybe it served a purpose in the past, but now it is a burden. Now it's holding you back and pulling you down from the kind of life you have to live. It's time to stop being crazy and stop when you remember this.

When you think about it, you just say, "This is fake."

Express your rejection in the worst way. Maybe you should say, "I'm stupid to think about it because it's a wrong memory. That is not real. I will stop being stupid. "Something like that. You will get used to it at some point and stop. Because there's no point in wasting more emotional resources on things that haven't happened yet.

CHAPTER SIX

Identify your excessive memory

After you identify your false memories and turn them off, the next step to take in a few weeks or even months is to focus on your excessive memories. This is a memory that actually happened.

People are there. You can confirm for yourself that this is really happening. There is evidence that this has happened. Nobody can deny that these things really did not happen.

The problem, however, is that you have done too much detail. In other words, you blow it up disproportionately. You are exaggerating things.

So, something that can happen to other people and they can reduce it or blow it up,

You decide to hang out, blow it up and give it a very poisonous meaning that it still bothers you today. This is excessive memory. Feel each excessive memory individually. Put yourself as much as possible in situations where this excessive memory has arisen.

Put yourself in the scene.

Imagine yourself in this place. Zero in fact as you know. This is just a fact okay and not your interpretation.

Please understand that these are two very different things. Focus on the facts about how they occur. Write down facts that oppose interpretation. Analyze what happened to you, record it as fast as you can, what actually happened and what you think happened and what you thought it meant.

Please understand that this is a reaction. This is an interpretation.

Write a long list of all your interpretations

Personal interpretation and analysis change over time. As we mature and change, our interpretations of things change. So just think of the long laundry list.

Choose interpretations that empower you

There are many ways to interpret a situation. There are many ways to see it.

Many committed suicide. Many feel depressed, small, weak and helpless. Many that fit your personal story of being a victim. This is a negative interpretation.

Choose a long list of interpretations from this experience that makes you feel empowered. This is the interpretation that makes you feel you have control over your life or that there is something left for tomorrow. In other words, there is a way out or an opportunity for hope. This is a positive interpretation.

Kill your negative interpretations by understanding their nature

Look at your negative interpretation of past memories and ask yourself: "Am I exaggerating? Am I just exaggerating them? Am I reading too much meaning to things?

Because whenever I read about what happened to me doesn't help me now. This interpretation is of no use to me. "Use this analysis to clear your list of interpretations of what actually happened. The remaining interpretations are maintained.

Give relevant interpretations

While your interpretation of empowerment is based on facts, you are not dealing with self-acceptance, self-hypnosis, or the like. Instead, you support your interpretation of the facts. But you must see your positive interpretation and realize it.

Are they directly related to experience? Do they flow directly from experience? If so, strengthen them. Because you have to understand that having a positive experience can be a breakthrough.

Instead of something that makes you small, weak, helpless, ugly, disgusting, stupid, senseless or whatever, you can use this experience as something that is a breakthrough for personal strength, autonomy, power, wisdom, beauty, transformation and hope. This is all about perspective.

But you must base this transition perspective from being positive or just good to being very positive on facts. So go back to the facts of this experience and say, for example: "My father left my mother even before I was born. This experience allowed me to be a more independent person, to always be grateful for what I have and to work hard for everything I have. "If this sounds familiar to you, this is the story of LeBron James.

Do yourself a favor, see what happens, and try to win there by seeing the positive impression you have to make it shine. Underline this. Test your mindset by constantly thinking about excessive memories. When you think of this excessive memory, you automatically focus on positivity.

However, this becomes a habit. Because when you think of these memories before, you blow them up disproportionately in a very negative way.

You feel like trash. You feel weak. You feel sick. You feel good now. But they are still the same basic facts. But you have to understand that what doesn't kill you makes you stronger. Sure, that might look devastating at the time, but actually that's the urge you need.

For example, a girl whose mother told her that she was ugly became a supermodel. Why? Because she wants to prove that her mother was wrong. It's not a luxury for everyone to say that she's beautiful, so she learnt to be more confident based on other things that enhance her natural beauty.

Let's clarify one thing here. There are all kinds of people in the world who will only have it for you. Somehow they misunderstand you and they decided to make your life like hell. At least they will tell you that they don't like you. Fair enough.

The truth is that just because other people say certain words or actions to hurt you does not mean they will hurt you. In short, Elinor Roosevelt said: "There is no one in this world who can make you feel disgusted without your permission."

It doesn't matter if you feel depressed, ugly, disgusting, stupid, mean, dirty or embarrassing. These are all interpretations. You don't have to accept their "gift". You don't have to let them reach you because in the end you are in control.

Either you control them or they control you. Do you see being in control as a good decision? Learn to take control of things. Take responsibility for your actions and end results. It might not be easy, it might be uncomfortable, but it's very important.

Chapter 7

Mindfulness

You need to practice with the notion that you can change that you always know. They are not inclined towards the past and are not burdened by fear of the future. Instead, focus on what is really happening here. Then focus on reality when it is revealed.

Different Mindfulness patterns for different people

Different people have different preferences regarding their attitudes. Some people deal well with certain types of meditation and awareness, while others lack. The key is to avoid thinking that there is a one size solution for all.

Instead, check and try the various attention options that I will give below. Please understand that this is not a complete list. There are many different options available to you and also various unique ways to achieve treatment. I only give you this as a sample. Once you are familiar with these techniques or chosen one that suits you, you might want to take things to the next level and look at other attention or meditation related choices.

Current observation meditation

This method is also called "single object monitoring". If you practice "observation meditation now", just look at the topic in front of you. What makes this type of meditation or mindfulness practice so powerful is that you put all your sensory efforts on this object. When you focus on texture, color, shape, and all the other descriptive dimensions of the object in front of you, don't think about childhood trauma.

You don't think about things that you normally worry about. You are certainly not afraid. Instead, you only allow your mind to focus all of its power on something that exists before you, here, now. It directs you to the present moment and helps you build a large amount of mental, emotional and physical discipline. Good is that not it?

Awakening meditation

Also known as "practicing meditation", this is one of the most practical meditation / attention techniques.

"Walking meditation" or "awakening meditation" means you can present yourself fully in one meditation. An outdoor environment with all sights, sounds, smells, tastes and textures. In other words you have full opportunity to fully live at a certain time and place.

If you make all these inputs, let yourself be locked in a moment and your mind will not wander. Of course, you go, but your focus is in line with you. This is the best way to mentally utilize your property.

This creates extraordinary discipline as you continue to shift your focus. This also allows you to be outside and interact with nature, but on your own terms. So this is a very powerful form of meditation practice. And that is also very practical. Then don't lock yourself behind closed doors, don't accept lotus sessions, and don't even close your eyes. Instead, you are outside and living your life to the full.

Transcendental Meditation

This technique uses mute spells. "Transcendental Meditation" has a terrible sound because of the word "transcendent". Many people are not very comfortable with religion. It does not suit them.

I see. Fair enough. But please remember that transcendental meditation uses silent mantras that don't mean anything. Mantras in Buddhism or Hindu traditions are meant to mean something. This is not one of them. This is just a repeated expression that allows you to accelerate breathing so that you can follow your thoughts rhythmically.

Transcendental meditation is very powerful because it's a that allows you to create a rhythm of awareness within you that allows you to destroy the mind. When done correctly, transcendental meditation does not stimulate the mind. How strong is that?

You suffer from anxiety because almost every other thought you have is frightening, disturbing, or frightening. There is only one thing for every thought that contributes to your fears, from the past, from the future, or from your worries about others.

Transcendental meditation is the opposite of that. That's 180 degrees of imagination, fear, doubt, anger or emotion. How can it be? You do not believe that.

The mind disappears through transcendental meditation. You can't even begin to have emotional effects because they don't even manifest. Such is the strength of transcendental meditation.

And the best thing about it?

That is easy. You just repeat your mute spell and sink inside. However, your mind starts to evaporate faster than ever. And before you know it, they aren't even formed.

Very interesting thing. In fact, many people report numbness in the limbs because they are free from physical and mental attachments.

You don't always have to feel in control. You don't have to prove yourself. No need to roam. Such is strong transcendental meditation.

Count your breath

This technique allows you to watch your mind from above. If you count your breath, you will eventually be able to clear your mind. It's as if you are sitting and watching clouds rolling in the sky. For certain dark clouds, if you look at it long enough you will find that they move slowly. Eventually they will really master your mind with enough time.

If you learn how to count your breath and acknowledge your thoughts, in the end they will just escape you. If you learn to breathe correctly, you only need to acknowledge your thoughts. You do not reject it. Don't sweep them under the carpet. Only acknowledge that they exist and then let them go.

You don't take advantage of them, you don't try to narrow them down to terms you can understand, you don't try to conquer them, you don't try to deal with them - you don't do all this. These are things that you usually do and that is why you are worried. That is why you are surrounded by all kinds of negative emotions such as feelings of guilt, regret, and nonsense.

If you count the breath instead, you still have that thought because you have acknowledged that it is a part of yourself, but you let it happen only to be replaced by other thoughts. And you let it happen. Before you realize it, you will be able to think of certain things without having to improve yourself and feel emotional. This alone makes it useful to incorporate your breathing-conscious training into your daily life.

Whatever type of meditation or attention you choose, choose one. You will do a good service for yourself when dealing with your fear constantly and continuously.

Chapter 8

Practicing into Perfection

If you don't feel it, it isn't real. Everything I teach here is useless if you keep it in your head. You have to act on it. You have to practice it because you will get reactions from all over the world.

The truth is how the world reacts is not very important. What's important is how you react to their reactions. So you know if you are an adult. So you know if you change. This is scary because you are now active and not just lying down and passively accepting what the world gives you. But you have to understand that the more you try, the better you do it.

You have to work with emotional urgency.

Overcome your fears by changing the way you process stimuli from the outside world and your connection to the past brings extraordinary benefits.

If you are still left feeling unclear, or if you don't really focus on the things you need to win, delay the script. Try to get emotional urgency by getting worse if you don't change the way you work. If you think things are bad now, wait for your fears to get worse.

Focus on loss, debilitating doubt, feeling of helplessness. Are they enough to encourage you to put one foot in front of the other as you walk towards life without fear? Use inertia. If you do something repeatedly, you are better. You can bring it to the bank. This is not a theory. This is not speculation. That's the reality.

Whether you talk about trade, school, relationships or whatever, if you keep doing something, you will get better. You will understand it, you will understand the nuances and eventually you will understand and become more successful at it. So stay here.

Treat yourself with good motivational encouragement

I have a secret to give myself a good push; to motivate me when I feel like I'm exhausted, when I try to change my view of the world and how I deal with my fears and anxieties.

Right now I am reading my personal travel diary and looking at my first day and comparing how I felt and thought that day with what I feel and think now. Believe me, it only gives me so much hope and gives me so much motivation. That reminds me that I have made some progress. I am not a sad case that cannot be changed. I can hope for a change. So do it. And it doesn't matter if you just start on the first day and then compare entries on the fifth day. There are some changes. You may have to look for it, maybe small, but this small change is hope.

Get an ally

Humans are social animals. We get things done much better when we are with other people. We do it much better when we help others.

Do yourself a favor, let someone help you. This is your ally. It could be your girlfriend, boyfriend, partner or parents. Whoever it is must be someone who loves you. Basically, this person will go with you during your trip.

Let your allies take care of you

The foundation of the system that I teach you in this book is honesty and sincerity. In other words, to overcome your negative thoughts and self-programming, you must be honest with yourself. Unfortunately it's very easy for us to lie to ourselves. It's easy for us to buy our own hopes.

Well, you have to give your allies permission to look after you. In general, you must give them permission to hurt your feelings. What we say is not true. We are lying to ourselves. It hurts to hear, but it is absolutely necessary. Give this person permission to help you properly.

Always check your personal story

Everyone has a story. Everyone has this hidden scenario, which is our life story that we tell ourselves. We say, "Oh, I'm poor" or "I'm stupid" or "I can't do it" or "That's me". Things like that. Well, those are the things that are holding us back. And it is very important to look at your personal scenario based on your knowledge of your thoughts and your past and your concerns about the future.

Let yourself feel good. If you change your mind and see the change, apply it. Say, "That's a good thing. I made progress. I have the right to be happy about that."

One of the most common and most frustrating things about anxiety is that you never let yourself feel happy. They never let you feel you are doing the right thing.

If you see a big change and your allies tell you that there is a big change, celebrate. Take him or her out for lunch. Think about what you have achieved. That is a milestone because before you were someone else. You are now one step closer to the person you want to be.

Conclusion

The information I have given you in this book is not useful unless you use it. You need to take action on these ingredients. You have to take action today. You have to face it.

This is not one of those things where you can enter, jump with both feet, and give up after a few weeks. This is a lifetime thing. Because if you pay more attention to the things that you want to think about, you start thinking about the right things.

You begin to think about your life so you can feel happy, satisfied, and victorious. Because at some point everything will collapse because you feel stronger. This is the life you have chosen, not the life someone has forced on you. Not the life that a random lottery puts on your lap. In other words, you begin to live a strong and responsible life.

Work tool 1

EAT

How to get rid of fear

Step 1: conduct an independent audit

Name all the things that make you afraid. Write down everything you fear. Mention the things that you have to blame. Write down the things that you are doubtful about and write them in your head.

Step 2: prioritize your list

Sort your list by intensity. Do this for everything that you have registered. Take your time to get this done.

Step 3: categorize your anxiety challenges

Begin to categorize yourself with the strongest fears. Categorize all your problems. Feel free to write down the same fears among various fields. Write down the intensity of the fear that you are sharing. Topic and ranking

Step 4: sure you can win

If you believe you will achieve it, you will. Remember: your life is a product of your thinking

Step 5: understand that the future starts with you

You must be committed to changing your mindset. Remember: changing your mindset is not an easy task. Dedicate yourself to thinking and changing your mindset. Make a series of confirmations. Start a personal change log.

I recommend this project every day to change your mindset.). Challenge your thoughts every day. Make a list of changes in your thinking. Victory is about consistency and endurance.

Step 6: take your past

Stop being determined by your past. Remember: the past is the past and gone forever.

Dealing with the last chapter. Ask yourself if the past trauma that you remember actually happened. Eliminate the wrong experience that you have.

Step 7: exaggerate excessive memories

Identify your excessive memory. Feel each excessive memory individually. Write down facts that oppose interpretation.

Choose interpretations that empower you. Kill your negative interpretations by understanding their nature.

Give relevant interpretations

Step 8: practice mindfulness

You have to adopt an awareness exercise that you will change and will always change your ways.

He acknowledged his thoughts

Current observation meditation

Awakening meditation

Transcendental Meditation

Breath Count / (Look at your mind from above.)

Step 9: practice, practice, practice

If you don't feel it, it isn't real. Get a feeling of emotional urgency

Use inertia

Treat yourself with good motivational encouragement

Step 10: adopt some best practices for self-directed natural anxiety solutions

Get an ally. Let your allies take care of you

Always check your personal story. Let yourself feel good at all times.

Overcome fear

How to stop fighting and start living

THINKING CARDS

Perform an independent audit. Name all the things that make you afraid. Write down everything you fear. Mention the things that you have to blame

Write down things that you doubt

Write it at the top of your head

Don't edit it

Take the time to write a complete list

Prioritize your list

Sort your list by intensity

Give yourself time to measure your intensity correctly, honestly. Categorize your anxiety challenges. Begin to categorize yourself with the strongest fears. Categorize all your problems.

Write them down and classify the intensity of fear that you have divided into several topics.

Think you can win?

If you believe you will achieve it. Faith is the foundation of your life. Your life is a product of your thinking, so think positively.

When you blame others, you give them authority and responsibility for their lives. The future starts with Y-O-U and Y-O-U alone.

You must be committed to changing your mindset. Changing your mindset is not an easy thing to do, but it must be done.

Dedicate yourself to thinking and changing your mind. Make a series of confirmations. Start a personal change log.

Recommend this project every day to change your mindset. Challenge your thoughts every day. Make a list of changes in your thinking. Victory is about consistency and endurance.

Perception of the past

Stop being determined by your past. The Past is past and long gone.

Dealing with the last chapter

Eliminate the wrong experience. That is not negative

Overcome excessive memory

Identify your excessive memory

Feel each excessive memory individually

Write down facts that oppose interpretation. Write a long list of all your interpretations

Choose interpretations that empower you

Kill your negative interpretations by understanding their nature. Play your interpretation of empowerment

Practice mindfulness

You need to practice the attention that you can change and that you always know

Settings

Different attention patterns for different people

Current observation meditation

Awakening meditation

Transcendental Meditation

Breath counts / Watch your mind from above

Practice to be perfect

If you don't feel it, it isn't real

Use inertia

Treat yourself with good motivational encouragement

Adoption of best practices for natural and independent anxiety solutions

Get an ally

Let your allies take care of you

Always check your personal story

Let yourself feel good

Overcome fear

How to stop fighting and start living

RESOURCES REPORT

LIST OF RESOURCES

Self-assessment resource

List of things that make you afraid (general)

List of things that concern you (specifically)

List the things that you fear

List of DUBTI matters

List of things you see

List of qualities

- Remove the top of your head.

- Don't edit your list.

- don't explain, just register.

- Take enough time to write a long list

Ranking list Ranking list

Read your list and sort by intensity - are the emotions intense?

- Are your feelings clear?

- Do they evoke memories?

If you answered YES to the above three, rank emotions higher.

Best practices

- Give yourself a long time - Be honest

Categorize your anxiety challenges

Intensity list

Vitality of memories

Your tendency to "lose" when you are caught in this thought

A simple "categorization trick" with which you can draw associations and connect the dots

- Solid and solid to see patterns

- free association

- Don't judge your association about the right to make mistakes.

Self-test beliefs

- what do you believe about your identity?

- what do you believe about your skills?

- What do you think about your life line?

- What do you think about your parents?

- What do you think about your job / career / boss?

- What do you believe in your relationship?

What does your belief say?

- your strength.

- Your ability to do things.

- Your ability to forgive.

- Your ability to start from scratch.

Choose beliefs that empower you.

- Start with the results.

- Keep an eye on your current thinking. YOU MUST use it for positive results.

www.ingramcontent.com/pod-product-compliance
Lightning Source LLC
Chambersburg PA
CBHW071550150726
48000CB00002B/1000